LEARNING ABOUT THE EARTH

Wetlands

by Hollie Endres

BLASTOFF! READERS 3

BELLWETHER MEDIA • MINNEAPOLIS, MN

Note to Librarians, Teachers, and Parents:

Blastoff! Readers are carefully developed by literacy experts and combine standards-based content with developmentally-appropriate text.

Level 1 provides the most support through repetition of high-frequency words, light text, predictable sentence patterns, and strong visual support.

Level 2 offers early readers a bit more challenge through varied simple sentences, increased text load, and less repetition of high frequency words.

Level 3 advances early-fluent readers toward fluency through increased text and concept load, less reliance on visuals, longer sentences, and more literary language.

Level 4 builds reading stamina by providing more text per page, increased use of punctuation, greater variation in sentence patterns, and increasingly challenging vocabulary.

Level 5 encourages children to move from "learning to read" to "reading to learn" by providing even more text, varied writing styles, and less familiar topics.

Whichever book is right for your reader, Blastoff! Readers are the perfect books to build confidence and encourage a love of reading that will last a lifetime!

This edition first published in 2008 by Bellwether Media.

No part of this publication may be reproduced in whole or in part without written permission of the publisher. For information regarding permission, write to Bellwether Media Inc., Attention: Permissions Department, Post Office Box 1C, Minnetonka, MN 55345-9998.

Library of Congress Cataloging-in-Publication Data
Endres, Hollie J.
    Wetlands / by Hollie Endres.
      p. cm. — (Blastoff! readers : learning about the earth)
Summary: "Simple text and supportive images introduce beginning readers to the physical characteristics and geographic locations of wetlands"—Provided by publisher.
    Includes bibliographical references and index.
    ISBN-13: 978-1-60014-116-4 (hardcover : alk. paper)
    ISBN-10: 1-60014-116-1 (hardcover : alk. paper)
    1. Wetlands—Juvenile literature. I. Title.

QH87.3.E53 2008
578.768—dc22
                                                    2007017569

Contents

Wetlands are places where the ground is wet and soggy most of the year.

Some wetlands
are as small as a
backyard. Other
wetlands cover
huge areas of land.

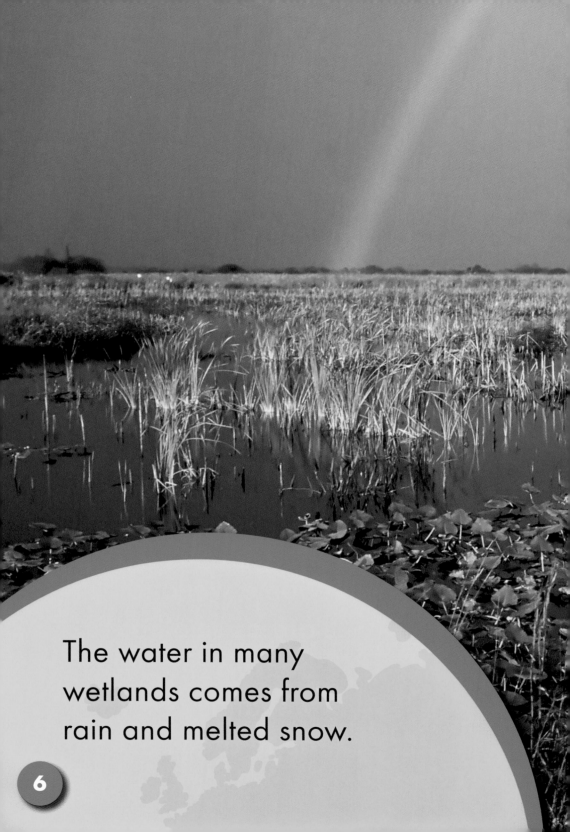

The water in many
wetlands comes from
rain and melted snow.

Sometimes water rises up from underground.

Sometimes water drains into wetlands from rivers and lakes.

Wetlands can form where a river meets the ocean. The level of water in these wetlands rises and falls with the **tide**.

Some wetlands are underwater
all year long.

Some wetlands dry up for part
of the year.

There are many kinds of wetlands. A **marsh** is open land that is covered by shallow water most of the time. Grassy plants grow in marshes.

Freshwater marshes form by lakes, rivers, and streams. Saltwater marshes form where fresh water flows into the ocean.

A **swamp** is an area of soggy land where trees grow. Swamps lie along the coast or near slow-moving rivers. Water floods swamps for only part of the year.

Over time, some ponds and lakes become **bogs**. Plants die and rot to make a thick mat called **peat** on top of the water. The peat sinks and fills in the pond or lake.

Many animals live in wetlands. Dragonflies, mosquitoes, and thousands of other insects fill the air. Fish lay eggs in shallow wetland water.

Beavers use trees and mud to build dams. Turtles and frogs live both in water and on land. Alligators live in warm wetland areas.

Ducks and other birds nest in wetlands. Birds that **migrate** long distances stop in wetlands to rest and find food.

Wetlands are important to people.
Water in some wetlands sinks into
the ground. People dig **wells**
to find this water. They drink it
and use it to water crops.

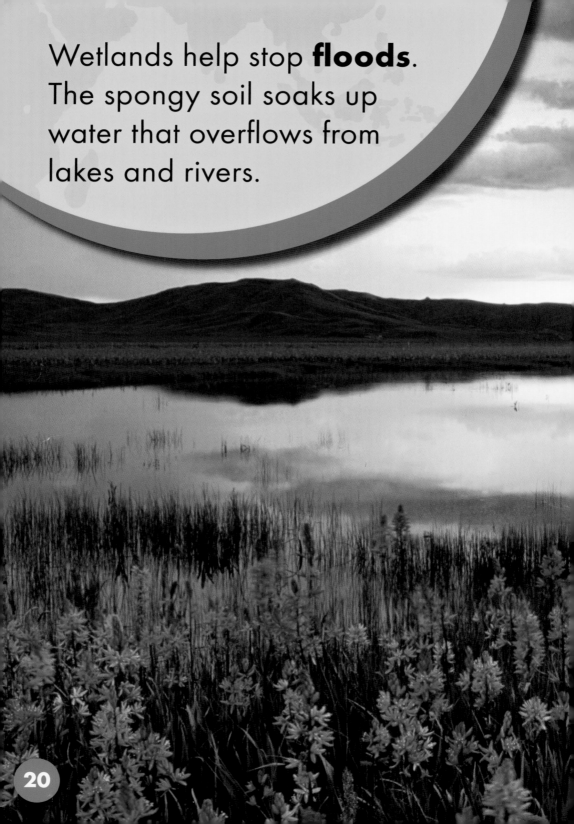

Wetlands help stop **floods**. The spongy soil soaks up water that overflows from lakes and rivers.

Wetlands also catch **pollutants** from factories, farms, and mines. Wetland soil and plants soak up the pollutants. This helps keep our water clean.

21

Glossary

bog—a type of wetland with wet and spongy land; bogs are peat covered with moss and other plants.

flood—water from a lake, river, or ocean on normally dry land

marsh—a type of wetland where grassy plants cover the land; marshes are almost always covered with water.

migrate—to go to a different place at the same time each year; many birds migrate south to live in warm areas during the winter; they fly north in the spring.

peat—rotted plants that have collected in wetlands over a long time

pollutant—something that makes air, water, or soil dirty

swamp—a type of wetland where trees grow and water floods the land part of the year

tide—the change in sea level caused by the pull of the Sun and the Moon on Earth; water covers the shore when the tide is in; the shore is uncovered when the tide is out.

well—a hole dug to reach underground water

To Learn More

AT THE LIBRARY

Fredericks, Anthony D. *Near One Cattail: Turtles, Logs, and Leaping Frogs.* Nevada City, Calif.: Dawn Publications, 2005.

Galko, Francine. *Wetland Animals.* Chicago, Ill.: Heinemann, 2003.

Kalman, Bobbie. *What Are Wetlands?* New York: Crabtree Publishing. 2003.

Sayres, Meghan Nuttall. *The Shape of Betts Meadow: A Wetlands Story.* Brookfield, Conn.: Millbrook Press, 2002.

Silver, Donald M. *Swamp.* New York: Learning Triangle Press, 1997.

Yolen, Jane. *Welcome to the River of Grass.* New York: Putnam, 2001.

ON THE WEB
Learning more about wetlands is as easy as 1, 2, 3.

1. Go to www.factsurfer.com

2. Enter "wetlands" into search box.

3. Click the "Surf" button and you will see a list of related web sites.

With factsurfer.com, finding more information is just a click away.

Index

The photographs in this book are reproduced through the courtesy of: Vera Bogaerts, front cover, pp. 4-5; CoverStock, pp. 6-7, 18; Tom Bean/Getty Images, p. 8; Cameron Davidson/Getty Images, p. 9; Getty Images, p. 10; Tom Mihalek/Getty Images, p. 11; Peter Blottman, p. 12; Norbert Rosing/Getty Images, p. 13; Romeo Koitmae, pp. 14-15; Hwang Soo Ping, p. 16; Stephen Frink Collection/Alamy, p. 17; Stephen McSweeny, p. 19; Steve Bly/Getty Images, pp. 20-21.